CATS

Quotes and Stuff

summersdale

Summersdale Publishers Ltd
46 West Street
Chichester
West Sussex
PO19 1RP
UK

www.summersdale.com

ISBN 184024 371 6

Printed and bound in Italy.
Cover photograph © Tim Flach/Getty Images

Illustrations by Kate Taylor

CONTENTS

INTRODUCTION

When did you last take the time to appreciate the majestic entity that deigns to stalk your house? Cats, those noble beasts who can just as easily snub you as love you, have long been the darlings of the literary world. Immortalised in poems, adored by the rich and famous and envied by dogs the world over, cats have shaped entire civilisations. At least, so they would have us believe...

Still unsure as to how to proceed, or just plain unconvinced? This book provides inspiration for any looking to improve their relationship with their furry companion, and a wake-up call to anyone who dares style themselves a cat 'owner'.

QUOTES

Of all God's creatures there is only one
that cannot be made the slave of the lash.
That one is the cat. If man could be
crossed with the cat it would improve the
man, but it would deteriorate the cat.

Mark Twain

Cats do not have to be shown how
to have a good time, for they are
unfailing ingenious in that respect.

James Mason

I've met many thinkers and many
cats, but the wisdom of cats
is infinitely superior.

Hippolyte Taine

After scolding one's cat one looks into
its face and is seized by the ugly
suspicion that it understood every word.
And has filed it for reference.

Charlotte Gray

Thousands of years ago, cats were
worshipped as gods. Cats have
never forgotten this.

Anonymous

Meow is like aloha - it
can mean anything.

Hank Ketchum

How we behave toward
cats here below determines
our status in heaven.

Robert A. Heinlein

As anyone who has ever been around a
cat for any length of time well knows
cats have enormous patience with the
limitations of the human mind.

Cleveland Amory

A cat has absolute emotional honesty:
human beings, for one reason or
another, may hide their feelings, but a
cat does not.

Ernest Hemingway

The smallest feline is a masterpiece.

Leonardo da Vinci

In the beginning, God created man,
but seeing him so feeble,
He gave him the cat.

Warren Eckstein

Most beds sleep up to six cats.
Ten cats without the owner.

Stephen Baker

Even overweight cats instinctively know
the cardinal rule: when fat, arrange
yourself in slim poses.

John Weitz

People that hate cats will come back
as mice in their next life.

Faith Resnick

There are many intelligent species in the universe. They are all owned by cats.

Anonymous

If I die before my cat, I want a little of
my ashes put in his food
so I can live inside him.

Drew Barrymore

Civilisation is defined by the
presence of cats.

Anonymous

The cat could very well be man's best
friend but would never
stoop to admitting it.

Doug Larson

Way down deep we are all
motivated by the same urges.
Cats have the courage to live by them.

Jim Davis

If you want to know the character
of a man, find out what
his cat thinks of him.

Anonymous

A cat is there when you call her -
if she doesn't have
something better to do.

Bill Adler

All cats like being the
focus of attention.

Peter Gray

Women and cats will do as they please,
and men and dogs should relax
and get used to the idea.

Robert A. Heinlein

Cats are living adornments.

Edwin Lent

For me, one of the pleasures of cats'
company is their devotion
to bodily comfort.

Sir Compton Mackenzie

30

The cat does not offer services. The cat
offers itself. Of course he wants care
and shelter. You don't buy love for
nothing. Like all pure creatures,
cats are practical.

William S. Burroughs

If it's raining at the back door,
every cat is convinced there's
a good chance that it won't
be raining at the front door.

William Toms

You own a dog but
you feed a cat.

Jenny de Vries

Even the stupidest cat
seems to know more
than any dog.

Eleanor Clark

There are no ordinary cats.

Colette

Cat's motto: No matter what you've
done wrong, always try to make
it look like the dog did it.

Anonymous

A cat's got her own opinion of human beings. She don't say much, but you can tell enough to make you anxious not to hear the whole of it.

Jerome K. Jerome

No matter how much
cats fight, there always seems to be
plenty of kittens.

Abraham Lincoln

What greater gift than
the love of a cat?

Charles Dickens

To err is human,
to purr feline.

Robert Byrne

PROVERBS

You will always be lucky if you know
how to make friends with strange cats.

Colonial proverb

In a cat's eye, all
things belong to cats.

English proverb

Beware of people
who dislike cats.

Irish proverb

After dark all
cats are leopards.

Native American proverb

Happy owner, happy cat.
Indifferent owner, reclusive cat.

Chinese proverb

A cat has nine lives. For three he plays,
for three he strays, and for
the last three he stays.

English proverb

Happy is the home with
at least one cat.

Italian proverb

The cat was created when
the lion sneezed.

Arabian proverb

Curiosity killed the cat,
satisfaction brought it back.

English proverb

I gave an order to a cat, and
the cat gave it to its tail.

Chinese proverb

Cats, flies and women
are ever at their toilets.

French proverb

Honest as the cat when
the meat's out of reach.

Old English proverb

A cat's eyes are windows
enabling us to see
into another world.

Irish legend

When the cat's away,
the mice will play.

Folk saying

A cat is a lion in a jungle
of small bushes.

Indian proverb

POETRY

Pussy can sit by the fire and sing

Pussy can sit by the fire and sing,
Pussy can climb a tree
Or play with a silly old cork and string
To 'muse herself, not me.
But I like Binkie my dog, because
He knows how to behave;
So, Binkie's the same as the First Friend was,
And I am the Man in the Cave!

Pussy will play Man Friday till
It's time to wet her paw
and make her walk on the windowsill
(For the footprint Crusoe saw);

Then she fluffles her tail and mews,
And scratches and won't attend
But Binkie will play whatever I choose,
And he is my true First Friend.

Pussy will rub my knees with her head
Pretending she loves me hard;
But the very minute I go to my bed
Pussy runs out in the yard,
And there she stays till the morning-light;
So I know it is only pretend
But Binkie, he snores at my feet all night,
And he is my Firstest Friend!

Rudyard Kipling

Cats are Wonderful Friends

Gentle eyes that see so much,
paws that have the quiet touch,
Purrs to signal 'all is well'
and show more love than words could tell.
Graceful movements touched with pride,
a calming presence by our side
A friendship that takes time to grow
Small wonder why we love them so.

Anonymous

Pangur Ban

I and Pangur Ban, my cat,
'Tis a like task we are at;
Hunting mice is his delight,
Hunting words I sit all night.

Oftentimes a mouse will stray
Into the hero Pangur's way;
Oftentimes my keen thought set
Takes a meaning in its net.

'Gainst the wall he sets his eye
Full and fierce and sharp and sly;
'Gainst the wall of knowledge I
All my little wisdom try.

When a mouse darts from its den,
O how glad is Pangur then!
O what gladness do I prove
When I solve the doubts I love.

So in peace our tasks we ply,
Pangur Ban, my cat, and I;
In our arts we find our bliss
I have mine and he has his.

Practice every day has made
Pangur perfect in his trade;
I get wisdom day and night,
Turning darkness into light.

Anonymous ninth-century monk

Black Cat

A cat as black
As blackest coal
Is out upon
His midnight stroll,
His steps are soft,
His walk is slow,
His eyes are gold,
They flash and glow.
And so I run
And so I duck,
I do not need
His black-cat luck.

Anonymous

Loving and Liking

Long may you love your pensioner mouse,
Though one of a tribe that torment the house:
Nor dislike for her cruel sport the cat,
Deadly foe both of mouse and rat;
Remember she follows the law of her kind,
And Instinct is neither wayward nor blind.
Then think of her beautiful gliding form,
Her tread that would scarcely crush a worm,
And her soothing song by the winter fire,
Soft as the dying throb of the lyre.

William Wordsworth

Kilkenny Cats

There once were two cats of Kilkenny,
Each thought there was one cat too many;
So they fought and they fit,
And they scratched and they bit,
Till, excepting their nails
And the tips of their tails,
Instead of two cats there weren't any.

Traditional

St Jerome's Cat

St Jerome in his study kept a great big cat,
It's always in his pictures, with its feet upon the mat.
Did he give it milk to drink, in a little dish?
When it came to Friday's, did he give it fish?
If I lost my little cat, I'd be sad without it;
I should ask St Jerome what to do about it.

I should ask St Jerome, just because of that,
For he's the only saint I know who kept a kitty cat.

Traditional English Nursery Rhyme

The Cat That Walked By Himself

He will kill mice, and he will be kind to babies
when he is in the house, just as long as they do not
pull his tail too hard. But when he has done that,
and between times, and when the moon gets up
and night comes, he is the Cat that walks by
himself, and all places are alike to him. Then he
goes out to the Wet Wild Woods or up the Wet
Wild Trees or on the Wet Wild Roofs, waving his
wild tail and walking by his wild lone.

Rudyard Kipling

The Owl and the Pussy-Cat

The Owl and the Pussy-cat went to sea
In a beautiful pea-green boat
They took some honey, and plenty of money,
Wrapped up in a five-pound note.
The Owl looked up to the stars above,
And sang to a small guitar,
'O lovely Pussy! O Pussy, my love,
What a beautiful Pussy you are,
You are,
You are!
What a beautiful Pussy you are!'

Edward Lear

SUPERSTITIONS

Dreaming of a white cat
means good luck.

American superstition

If a cat washes behind its ears,
it will rain.

English superstition

A strange black cat on your
porch brings prosperity.

Scottish superstition

When you see a one-eyed cat, spit on your thumb, stamp it in the palm of your hand, and make a wish. The wish will come true.

American superstition

A cat sneezing is a good omen for
everyone who hears it.

Italian superstition

A cat sleeping with all four paws
tucked under means
cold weather ahead.

English superstition

When moving to a new home, always
put the cat through the window instead
of the door, so that it will not leave.

American superstition

When a cat washes behind its ears,
you may expect visitors.

Dutch superstition

It is bad luck to cross a stream
carrying a cat.

French superstition

ONE-LINERS

Q: How can you tell when
a cat is happy?

A: It turns purrrple.

Q: What happens if a cat
eats your knitting?

A: She has mittens.

Q: What do you give a cat
with a sweet tooth?

A: Mice pudding with chocolate mouse.

Q: What purrs and does backflips?

A: An acrocat.

Q: Why did the little boy try to feed his pocket money to the cat?

A: Because he had been told to put money in the kitty.

Q: What do you get if you cross a cat and a duck?

A: A duck-filled catty-puss.

Q: What do you call a cat
with a little red book?

A: Chairman Miaow.

Q: Why is it good when your
cat loses its voice?

A: Because no mews is good mews.

Q: What happens if a cat loses its tail?

A: It goes for re-tail therapy.

Q: What do you get if you cross a cat
with some bandages?

A: A first aid kit.

HISTORICAL
CATS

The first White House cat was owned
by Abraham Lincoln. Other presidential
cats have included 'Misty Malarky Ying
Yang', a Siamese owned by Jimmy
Carter's daughter Amy, and 'Slippers',
Theodore Roosevelt's blue-grey cat that
had more than five toes on each paw.

A famous literary cat was Mysouff, owned by Alexander Dumas, the author of *The Three Musketeers*. Renowned for his feline intuition, he was able to predict what time Dumas would finish work, even if his master was working late into the night.

When Charles Dickens' cat had kittens,
he took them all from their mother save
one. Known as 'The Master's Cat', this
kitten would snuff out the author's
candle in order to get his attention.

Dr Albert Schweitzer, the 1952 Nobel Peace Prize Winner, became ambidextrous in order to accommodate his cat Sizi. Whenever Sizi fell asleep on the doctor's arm, he would obediently write prescriptions with his other hand to avoid waking her.

An Egyptian sultan in the thirteenth century left his entire fortune to the stray cats of Cairo, his legacy ensuring that for years to come homeless and impoverished cats were entitled to recieve a free daily meal.

90

The prophet Mohammed's love of cats
was sufficiently great to ensure the
comfort of his cat Muezza. It is said that
one day when he was being called to
prayer he cut off the sleeve of his robe
rather than disturb the sleeping cat.

Jock, the favourite orange tabby of Sir Winston Churchill, slept in his master's bed every night and attended wartime cabinet meetings. Churchill even comissioned a painting of him.

The Paris home of Swiss artist
Theophile Steinlen's was christened
'Cats Corner' due to his tendancy to
incorporate his beloved cats into most
of his designs.

Thou art the Great Cat, the avenger of the gods, and the judge of words, and the president of the sovereign chiefs and the governor of the holy Circle; thou art indeed...the Great Cat.

Inscription on the Royal Tombs at Thebes

The more I *see* of men,
the more I love my dog

Olivia Edward

www.summersdale.com